DOBERMAN PINSCHERS

Julie Fiedler

The Rosen Publishing Group's
PowerKids Press™
New York

For Michelle

Published in 2006 by The Rosen Publishing Group, Inc.
29 East 21st Street, New York, NY 10010

First Edition

Editor: Jennifer Way
Book Design: Elana Davidian

Photo Credits: Cover (left) © Royalty-Free/Corbis; Cover (right) © Daphne Godfrey Trust/Animals Animals; p. 4 (top) © Eunice Pearcy/Animals Animals; p. 4 (bottom) © Mitsuaki Iwago/Minden Pictures; pp. 7 (top), 19 (top) © Ralph Reinhold/Animals Animals; p. 7 (bottom) © Barbara Wright/Animals Animals; p. 8 Eric Lessing/Art Resource, NY; p. 11 © Bettmann/Corbis; p. 12 © Sean Murphy/Getty Images; p. 15 (top) © Mella Panzella/Animals Animals; p. 15 (bottom) © Carl & Ann Purcell/Corbis; p. 16 © IT Stock Int'l/Index Stock Imagery, Inc.; p. 19 (bottom) © Gerard Lacz/Animals Animals; p. 20 © Phil Martin/Index Stock Imagery, Inc.

Library of Congress Cataloging-in-Publication Data

Fiedler, Julie.
Doberman pinschers / Julie Fiedler.— 1st ed.
p. cm. — (Tough dogs)
Includes bibliographical references and index. ISBN 1-4042-3120-X (library binding)
1. Doberman pinscher. I. Title.

SF429.D6F54 2006
636.73'6—dc22
2004029523

Manufactured in the United States of America

Contents

Above: Doberman pinschers are popular guard dogs and police dogs. Because of the tough jobs Dobermans do, some people are afraid of them. Right: Doberman pinscher puppies are born with floppy ears. These are later cropped so that they stand up.

Meet the Doberman Pinscher

Doberman pinschers are a **breed** of dog known for their intelligence, strength, and **loyalty**. They are known around the world as some of the best guard dogs, and they are also loving pets. Some people have heard bad stories about them in the news and think that they are **dangerous**, but that is because they do not know the breed well. Doberman pinschers are very loyal and will protect their owners if they are in danger.

Doberman pinschers make wonderful working dogs or companions. They are full of energy and need to get lots of exercise through running and playing. They can take part in activities, such as tracking and hunting, which require a good sense of smell. They are very smart and need skilled owners who are willing to train them. A properly trained Doberman pinscher can be a joy to have as a pet and helper.

What a Doberman Pinscher Looks Like

Doberman pinschers can easily be recognized by their special markings and by their tall, lean bodies. They are medium sized and strong. They stand 24 to 28 inches (61–71 cm) tall and weigh 60 to 75 pounds (27–34 kg). They have broad chests and their tails are often bobbed, or cut, by their owners. Their ears are naturally floppy, but when they are puppies, their ears are often cropped, or cut, to be pointed. Cropping tails and ears is a matter of the owner's preference. Leaving ears and tails in their natural state has become more popular in recent years.

Doberman pinschers have long **muzzles**, which give their heads a triangular shape. Their eyes are almond shaped and are usually brown. Doberman pinschers have short, smooth coats, which are usually black with rust-colored markings on their muzzles, ears, feet, and chests. Some Doberman pinschers have red, blue, or fawn-colored coats, but those are less common than black.

Above: *This Doberman pinscher puppy has had its ears cropped and its tail docked.*
Left: *The adult Doberman pinscher here has the rust-colored face markings that make the breed so recognizable.*

This detail from an ancient Roman mosaic, or tile picture, shows one of the large working dogs that were common at that time. These dogs are believed to be one of the ancestors of today's working breeds, such as the Doberman pinscher.

8

Ancestors of the Doberman Pinscher

The common **ancestor** of dogs is the wolf. More than 15,000 years ago, wild dogs began to live with people and became **domesticated**. During that time dogs looked different from those we see today. Some of those ancient dogs were the ancestors of today's breeds.

The Doberman pinscher has the same ancestors as many of today's tough dogs, such as the Rottweiler. In ancient times Romans had a large breed of dog called a mastiff. These dogs were strong and were used in battle or as guard dogs. Around A.D. 74, the Romans occupied other parts of Europe, such as Germany and Britain. They brought these dogs with them for help guarding livestock and watching over their camps. When the Romans returned to Italy hundreds of years later, they left some of these dogs behind. Over the next thousand years, these dogs were **bred** with other dogs. The Doberman pinscher is one of the breeds that came from the Roman mastiffs.

History of the Doberman Pinscher

Doberman pinschers were first bred in Thuringia, Germany, in the 1880s by Karl Louis Dobermann. Dobermann decided to experiment with dog breeding in order to create a better watchdog. He wanted a fearless and strong dog. It is believed that he used several different breeds, including Manchester terriers, Weimaraners, and Rottweilers. Dobermann finally bred his dream dog. It was called Dobermann's dog by local residents and the Thuringian pinscher in other parts of Germany. This breed soon became known as the Doberman pinscher.

During the early 1900s, Doberman pinschers became popular across Europe and North America. They also became working dogs in the military. They help soldiers with jobs such as scouting and patrolling. A **statue** of a Doberman pinscher in Guam honors the brave dogs who died fighting in **World War II**. Today this breed can be found throughout the world.

Rollo, the Doberman pinscher in this photograph, served with the U.S. Marines in World War II. Doberman pinschers are popular with the military because they are brave and learn to do new tasks quickly.

Doberman pinschers, such as the one in this picture, have been winners at dog shows. Although they are known for being a tough breed, Doberman pinschers have been carefully bred over time to be more gentle. This was accomplished by choosing to breed the gentlest dogs together.

Doberman Pinschers Today

There were 11,500 Doberman pinschers listed with the American Kennel Club in 2004, making them one of the top 25 most popular breeds. They are valued for their grace and intelligence. Because of their strength, they are often used for work as guard dogs and for many uses with the police and military. Doberman pinschers have been trained to help control crowds, sniff out dangerous items such as drugs or bombs, and do patrol work. In addition to being trained as working dogs, Doberman pinschers make wonderful pets and can also be trained as show dogs.

Doberman pinschers are known for their loyalty and will keep their owners from harm. In the past the breed was more **aggressive**, but over time they have been bred to have a milder character. Because of Dobermans' long history as guard dogs, however, many people are afraid of this breed.

Tough Breed

Some people believe Doberman pinschers are naturally mean because they have seen them play attack dogs in movies or on television. There have also been news stories about aggressive Dobermans. The truth is that Doberman pinschers are not naturally mean.

Sadly the strength, loyalty, and bravery that make Doberman pinschers such good working dogs have been taken advantage of by bad owners. Owners who wish to use Doberman pinschers for guarding or police work should not train their dogs without the help of dog-training specialists. Some careless owners mistreat their Doberman pinschers or train them to attack. Owners should always have the safety of their dogs and other people in mind. They should be careful when raising them and take good care of their Doberman pinschers. A properly raised Doberman pinscher makes a loving pet.

Above: *When they are properly cared for and trained, a Doberman pinscher can be a happy and gentle pet.* Right: *Doberman pinschers that have been mistreated or trained to attack can pose a danger to people or other animals.*

It is important to bring Doberman pinscher puppies into contact with different people and settings, so they will not act aggressively out of fear. This is called socialization. It is also important to learn how to be safe around dogs. The family in this picture is carefully bringing this Doberman pinscher puppy into contact with children.

Caring for a Doberman Pinscher

It is important to care for dogs properly, no matter what breed they are. Good care requires providing shelter, healthy food and water, love, exercise, and **obedience** training to prevent bad **behavior**. Owners should groom their Doberman pinschers once a week by brushing their coat. This helps keep their coat shiny and their skin healthy. Owners must also make sure their dogs visit the **veterinarian** for regular checkups.

Doberman pinschers are very energetic. They are good dogs for active people who will give them lots of exercise. Like any dog they can behave badly if they do not get enough exercise and are not properly trained.

DOG SAFETY TIPS

- Never approach a dog you do not know.
- When approaching a dog, offer the back of your hand to the dog to sniff.
- Speak softly, not loudly. Move gently, not suddenly.
- Never try to pet a dog through a fence.
- Never bother a dog while it is sleeping, eating, or sick.
- Do not pull at a dog's fur, ears, or tail. Never tease or hit a dog.
- Never approach a dog that is growling or showing its teeth. Avoid eye contact with the dog and back away slowly. Yelling and running can cause the dog to chase you or act aggressively.

Doberman pinschers learn quickly and are very strong. For this reason it is important for owners to train their Doberman pinschers properly and to remain firm at all times. If owners do not stay in control, their Doberman pinschers may try to become the boss. If owners want help with basic training, they can take their dogs to obedience school. Doberman pinschers that work need special training to do their jobs.

Another important part of raising healthy Doberman pinschers is **socialization**. Socialization includes bringing young dogs into contact with different people, settings, and other dogs while watching them carefully. Adult Doberman pinschers are more likely to be well behaved if they are properly socialized when they are puppies. Like all dogs if Doberman pinschers do not have proper socialization, they might act aggressively out of fear and harm someone.

Above: *Properly socialized dogs can interact safely with other dogs and people.* **Right:** *This Doberman pinscher is running an obstacle course. Experts suggest exercising Doberman pinschers a few times each day for short periods.*

Doberman pinschers have done many heroic acts for their owners. They are also valued as police dogs because they are powerful, brave, and intelligent.

Heroic Doberman Pinschers

Through the years Doberman pinschers have become known for their brave work with the police and the military. There are also many Doberman pinschers that are heroic household pets. For example, in the 1990s, a pet Doberman pinscher named Sabbath helped save her owner Buddy, who was two years old. Buddy fell into a tub full of water and was drowning. Sabbath barked loudly until Buddy's father came to see what was wrong. He was able to save his son, thanks to Sabbath.

Another pet Doberman pinscher, named Tyler, saved his owner Jason in the 1990s. When Tyler noticed that Jason was gasping for breath during the night, he ran to wake up Jason's mother. Jason's mother was able to help her son because of Tyler's quick action.

These Doberman pinschers showed great intelligence and bravery. These stories show how Dobermans' problem-solving skills are helpful at work in the real world.

Doberman pinschers are an outstanding breed. Their loyalty, strength, bravery, and intelligence have made them popular around the world. Many Doberman pinschers are working dogs, and many are beloved pets.

A Doberman pinscher named Stormy was a great example of this breed. In 1979, a couple in Wyoming adopted Stormy. Stormy was very good at obedience training and was trained to be a search and rescue dog. His owners later decided to train him for **pet therapy** work, too. Stormy visited nursing homes and a local hospital to help brighten the lives of the patients. In 1984, the Cheyenne Health Care Center in Wyoming named Stormy Therapy Dog of the Year. Stormy was quite a dog!

People should respect this breed. Now that you know more about Doberman pinschers, you can help teach others about them.

Glossary

aggressive (uh-GREH-siv) Ready to fight.

ancestor (AN-ses-ter) A relative who lived long ago.

behavior (bee-HAY-vyur) Ways to act.

bred (BRED) To have brought a male and a female animal together so they will have babies.

breed (BREED) A group of animals that look alike and have the same relatives.

dangerous (DAYN-jeh-rus) Able to cause harm.

domesticated (duh-MES-tuh-kayt-ed) Raised to live with people.

loyalty (LOY-ul-tee) Faithfulness.

muzzles (MUH-zuhlz) Parts of animals' heads that come forward and include the nose.

obedience (oh-BEE-dee-ens) Willingness to do what you are told to do.

pet therapy (PEHT THEHR-uh-pee) When people use animals to help them deal with certain problems.

socialization (soh-shuh-luh-ZAY-shun) Learning to be friendly.

statue (STA-chyoo) An image of a person or an animal, usually cut in clay, metal, or stone.

veterinarian (veh-tuh-ruh-NER-ee-un) A doctor who treats animals.

World War II (WURLD WOR TOO) A war fought by the United States, Great Britain, France, and the Soviet Union against Germany, Japan, and Italy from 1939 to 1945.

Index

Web Sites

Due to the changing nature of Internet links, PowerKids Press has developed an online list of Web sites related to the subject of this book. This site is updated regularly. Please use this link to access the list:
www.powerkidslinks.com/tdog/doberman/